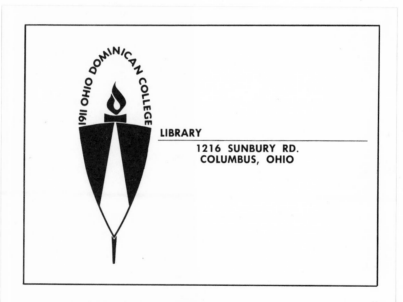

THE RUSSIAN REVOLUTION

The Russian Revolution may be traced from its roots in the nineteenth century, through the crises of 1905 and the First World War, to its climax in October, 1917, and beyond. The author of this book, Lionel Kochan, does this, illustrating his story with contemporary graphic material ranging from photographs to rare political cartoons. Dr. Kochan begins by tracing the gradual rise of revolutionary movements inside Russia. He evaluates the impact of changing conditions on the land and in the towns, and assesses the importance of the Russian middle class, the Duma, and the failures and achievements of political leaders like Sergei Witte, and of the last Tsar, Nicholas II. He tells how events in the early years of the twentieth century in Russia created an atmosphere of revolution—the war with Japan, the naval mutinies, the strikes, the strange influence of Rasputin—and shows how Lenin and others worked to create a new social order.

The hardship and chaos generated by the First World War spelled the downfall of the bankrupt Tsarist régime, which proved unable to contain the sequence of strikes and demonstrations that occurred early in 1917. Dr. Kochan discloses the complex political strife which followed the Tsar's abdication, and shows how Lenin's Bolsheviks and the Red Guards eventually overcame the moderate elements. The last sections of his book reveal how the often divided Bolsheviks consolidated their hold on Russia, and asserted their policies in the years of reconstruction and foreign isolation.

A PUTNAM PICTORIAL SOURCES BOOK

THE RUSSIAN REVOLUTION

LIONEL KOCHAN

G. P. PUTNAM'S SONS · NEW YORK

The Putnam Pictorial Sources Series

J
947
K

Frontispiece: The storming of the Kremlin in
Moscow during the 1917 Russian Revolution

Copyright © 1971 by Wayland (Publishers) Ltd
All rights reserved. This book, or parts thereof, must not be
reproduced in any form without permission
Published simultaneously in the Dominion of Canada by
Longmans Canada Limited, Toronto

Library of Congress Catalog Card Number: 73–147286

Printed in England

CONTENTS

CHAPTER ONE

WHEN DID IT BEGIN?

MOST PEOPLE, if asked when the Russian Revolution took place, would reply without hesitation: 1917. For that surely was the year when the first Bolshevik government was formed under the leadership of Lenin and Trotsky. All that is true, yet it is not a complete answer to the question. To see why, we must know something of Russian history before 1917. In fact, to understand what took place in 1917 one must look at certain features of the history of Russia in the whole century preceding the actual outbreak of revolution.

The achievement of the Bolsheviks in 1917 was to exploit feelings of dissatisfaction and revolt that had been growing ever stronger among many sections of Russian society. This applied particularly to the peasants. Since the peasants formed the bulk of the population their welfare was obviously of paramount importance. In fact, they were on the whole desperately poor, and barely able to survive from one harvest to the next. If the harvest was poor they might well face famine conditions. This mass poverty was not necessarily due to shortage of land. On the contrary, it was more likely to result from backward methods of agriculture. The Russian peasants produced much less than their counterparts in France or Germany who had perhaps less land at their disposal.

Another factor that weighed down on the Russian peasants was the vast increase in their numbers. The population of Russia exploded from 63 millions in 1867

to 92 millions in 1896. The amount of land at the peasants' disposal also increased, of course, but not in the same proportion. Here was another cause of peasant poverty. In 1905 a government report on the plight of the peasantry quite simply stated: "Very often the peasants do not have enough allotment land, and cannot during the year feed themselves, clothe themselves, heat their homes, maintain their tools and livestock, secure seed for sowing, and lastly, discharge all their taxes and obligations to the state, the zemstvo and the commune."

The government, aware of these conditions, was not inactive. Between 1906 and 1914, particularly, it tried to improve the standard of peasant agriculture by making loans available, by teaching new agricultural techniques, by moving surplus peasant families to Siberia, and by introducing co-operative systems of marketing and production. But the government's efforts were hampered by the outbreak of the First World War in 1914. In any case, their efforts did not entirely match up to the scale of the problem.

By this time another source of dissatisfaction was opening up before the government: this was the growth of an industrial working class. As Russia entered the early stages of a European-type industrial revolution, a new class of workers grew up. They worked in the new factories, mines and workshops of St. Petersburg (now Leningrad), Moscow, Warsaw, and the Ukraine. They suffered from all the hardships that workers had undergone in the Western world—low wages, poor housing, frequent accidents, and exploitation by their employers. By 1900 the workers still did not number much above a million, or about one per cent of the population. But since they were concentrated in a few major cities their importance was out of proportion to their actual numbers. Again, the government was not unaware of the workers' problems, but its response was half-hearted. It passed factory acts, as in Europe, to limit working hours and introduced accident and unemployment assurance. But all these efforts were on much too small a scale to make any real impact. As a result, the industrial history of Tsarist Russia in the late nineteenth and early twentieth centuries was marked by recurrent strikes and occasional armed conflicts between workers and police. These troubles reached a climax in July, 1914, when street fighting broke out in St. Petersburg itself.

It was because of conditions such as these that, towards the end of the nineteenth century, the government organized a sort of mobile police force in the industrial districts. This force was always ready to visit any trouble spot to intervene in case of a threatened clash between strikers and employers. As time passed, more and more use had to be made of this force.

Another means whereby the authorities attempted to control the workers' movement was through the organization of government sponsored trade unions. This would separate the economic aspirations of the workers from their political struggle. If it should prove possible to satisfy demands for improved working conditions and higher wages, then it might reasonably be hoped that the workers would be less attracted by the appeal of the revolutionaries. The unions organized in this way by the government did have some success at the turn of the century. But they were never anything more than a conventional experiment in labour relations and led to little permanent improvement in social conditions.

The workers, like the peasants, did not really blame the Tsar himself for their sufferings. It was always the fault of his officials or subordinates. This is one reason why, before 1917, the movement of revolt only once developed into an actual threat to the government. That was in 1905. For the rest of the time, Russia's poor communications, and the different rates at which peasants' and workers' movements grew, prevented any coordination between the two.

The Russian Empire was multinational: it contained many different peoples and religious groupings. Not only were there Christians of all denominations, Moslems and Jews; there were Poles, Ukrainians, Mongols, Tartars, Finns, and others. The Empire had its share of the nationalist strivings seen in the rest of

Europe, but in Russia, Polish and Finnish nationalism, for example, was ruthlessly repressed. The government tried to rule the subject peoples more and more centrally, to suppress their national culture, and even forcibly to convert them to Greek Orthodox Christianity. The result was yet another source of disaffection.

A policy of this sort might have worked if the government had been efficient. But this was far from being the case. Tsarism was an autocracy: that is to say, the Tsar was the supreme ruler. He was not responsible to any elected body (until 1906) and himself appointed state officials. However, he was certainly not bound to take their advice. In this system, much obviously depended on the personality and competence of each Tsar. Unfortunately, Nicholas II (1894–1917) was undoubtedly weaker than any of his nineteenth-century predecessors. First, although he took his duties very seriously, he was really more interested in his family life. He looked upon affairs of state as an unwelcome intrusion into the domestic circle of the Empress and their children. Second, Nicholas was an obstinate man. He was obsessed with keeping all the privileges of his position, and ignored the advice of his ministers. Third, he had no understanding of the new forces in his Empire, generated by nationalism and industrialization.

In normal circumstances these movements might have been tolerable, but for Russia at this time the circumstances were anything but normal. One reason was the recurrent wars in which the Empire found itself involved—the Crimean War (1854–56), the Russo-Turkish War (1877–78), the Russo-Japanese War (1904–5) and finally the First World War (1914–18). All these, and particularly the last, demanded an immense effort from the state which taxed its resources in materials and manpower. It is no accident that Russia was defeated in all these wars, except that against Turkey. But even here it had to yield at the conference table what it had won in the battlefield.

We can therefore understand why Russia was in a state of growing crisis during this period. Many people were aware of this situation, and the nineteenth century saw reformers of many viewpoints try to remodel the state. Their views ranged from mild reform to extreme radicalism involving assassination and armed revolt.

In 1917 all these factors came to a head. There was now a revolutionary situation involving every aspect of Russian society. In March, 1917, Nicholas II was forced to abdicate in favour of a liberal-minded provisional government. In November this fell in its turn to the Bolsheviks. Even now the Russian turmoil was not over, for two years of civil war followed. By the end of 1920, when some semblance of stability had returned, a very different Russia faced the world. A

Council of People's Commissars had replaced the Tsar and his cabinet; the Bolshevik party had acquired a monopoly of political life; private ownership of the means of production had been abolished. All these events had inspired the growth of a worldwide Communist movement that alarmed the capitalist world. The strength of Communism was much exaggerated. Nevertheless, the fact that it existed at all is dynamic testimony to the fact that the Russian Revolution was correctly seen as one of the major events of the twentieth century.

If the Russian Revolution can be said to begin anywhere, it is with the "Decembrist" revolt, so called because it took place in December, 1825. The leaders of the revolt were guard officers and the scions of highly placed families. Most had served with the Russian armies in western Europe during the Napoleonic Wars. Although their aims were confused, the Decembrists hoped to bring to Russia some form of Western constitutionalism. This would involve overthrowing the Tsarist autocracy, and replacing it by a republic or a constitutional monarchy. Pavel Pestel was one of their more radical leaders (1). Others, such as Sergey Muravyov (2), had more moderate aims. On their return to Russia after the Congress of Vienna (1815), the future Decembrists formed secret revolutionary societies. They thought they saw their chance in the confused period following the death of the Tsar

1

3

2

Alexander I in November, 1825. When the time came for their regiments to swear allegiance to the new Tsar, Nicholas I, the plotters marched their men to the Senate Square near the Winter Palace in St. Petersburg, where the ceremony was to take place. But their plan was confused, and for most of the day the mutineers were inactive (page 42). They neither took the oath nor launched any hostile action. Nicholas I tried to persuade the rebel commanders and their troops to disperse. Finally, when dusk fell, he ordered his artillery to fire and in this way cleared the square. Five of the ringleaders were hanged. Many others were imprisoned or exiled. Picture (3) shows Decembrists in prison. The episode had no immediate effect on Russian affairs. But it showed something of the dissatisfaction present amongst the higher levels of Russian society.

To Nicholas I, the new Tsar (4), the shock of the Decembrist revolt reinforced a temperament that was already imperious. Nicholas intended that nothing of the sort should happen again during his reign. He was anxious that schools and universities should be supervised, and not teach subversive doctrines. "Autocracy, nationality and orthodoxy"—these were the watchwords of his Minister of Education, Count Sergey Uvarov. Moreover,

Nicholas feared the example of what was happening outside Russia itself. In 1830 a rebellion broke out in Poland against Russian rule. A widespread campaign of suppression had to be made by the Russian army. The rebellion in Poland coincided with revolutions in France and Belgium, so that Nicholas was even more eager to prevent all contact between his own Empire and the Western world. The effectiveness of his measures was shown in 1848–49;

4

5

6

although political meetings took place in St. Petersburg and elsewhere (5) Russia remained all but immune to the revolutions that spread from France to nearly every country in central Europe. However, one episode did show that the voice of liberal opposition was not entirely stilled: this was what became known as the "Petrashevsky Conspiracy," named after its chief organizer. In essence, the conspiracy amounted to little more than occasional meetings at M. Butashevich Petrashevsky's apartment in St. Petersburg, where a group of intellectuals read the works of French Utopian Socialists. One of the outstanding members of the group was the great novelist, Dostoievsky (6). When the group was betrayed to the police by an informer, twenty-one of the participants were sentenced to death. Not until the last moment were their sentences commuted to imprisonment and exile.

However, the autocratic régime of Nicholas I was not as strong as it looked. Despite all his efforts to impose uniformity of political and religious belief, and to militarize the Empire, this repressive system at length came to disaster. The immediate cause lay in foreign policy. The Tsar had two chief aims: to block the spread of democracy and liberalism in Europe, and to acquire the Dardanelles and Constantinople. The second would give Russian ships free access to the eastern Mediterranean. But Nicholas I had overestimated Russian power. His Mediterranean ambitions involved Russia in the Crimean War (1854–56) in which the Empire found itself at war with France and Britain. In September, 1854, the Allied forces landed in the Crimea near Eupatoria and laid siege to Sebastopol (7). At Balaclava, where the British Light Brigade made their ill-fated charge, another famous

engagement took place (8). There was military inefficiency on both sides, but it was worse on the Russian. It soon became clear that not only did Russia lack the railways and communication facilities needed for a modern war, but that its armies were badly equipped and badly trained. The Russian generals even lacked good maps of the Crimean Peninsula. Nicholas I did not live to see Russia's final defeat. He died in March, 1855. His death was the occasion for a ceremonial funeral (9). But all the majesty could not hide the fact that his repressive system had died with him. Great changes would be needed in Russian life and outlook, if the Empire was to meet the challenges of the next half century. It was to this task that his successor Alexander II turned himself.

8

16 Alexander II (10) came to the throne in the midst of the Crimean War (11), and realized the need for certain reforms. Peasant unrest had reappeared in certain provinces. Serfdom was the greatest problem (serfs, who formed most of the population, were bound to their landowners' estates). Alexander declared that it was "better to abolish serfdom from above than to wait for it to begin to abolish itself from below"—in other words by revolution. Many landowners opposed Alexander's policy. But in 1861 the emancipation of all the serfs was proclaimed in each village square (12), though it left them burdened with debt. Other reforms of the "Tsar-Liberator" included a system of regular courts, and some local representative government in villages and towns. However, in the 1860s active popular discontent persuaded Alexander and his government to drop further efforts. This

10

11

disillusioned many thinking Russians about peaceful reform. These included Alexander Herzen (13), who vowed to avenge the Decembrists. Herzen clashed with the authorities, and was exiled from Moscow. Not only did he reject the autocracy; he came to despise capitalism and the middle-class outlook. In their place he extolled the virtues of the Russian peasant commune. When Alexander II announced his aim of freeing the serfs, Herzen gave him cautious support. In the journal *Kolokol* (*The Bell*), 1857–61, the exiled Herzen expressed these views and became politically influential. A commemorative medal was issued for Herzen and his journal in 1863 (14, 15). The half-hearted nature of the emancipation in 1861 was a bitter blow to Herzen. But it did not diminish his faith in the Russian peasantry, which was his main legacy to the revolutionary movement.

12

13

14

15

The full spectrum of revolutionary thought and activity would be incomplete without some mention of Mikhail Bakunin (1814–76) (16) and Nicholas Tchernishevsky (1828–89) (17). Bakunin was an anarchist; he worked for a revolution to destroy the state and split up society into its natural economic components. The peasants would own and enjoy the fruits of the land that they worked themselves (18), and industrial workers would possess the workshops and factories which belonged to their employers. Picture (19), drawn in 1861, shows a group of Russian peasants. Bakunin led an adventurous life. His revolutionary activities, for example, led to his exile in Siberia. But he managed to secure a post in the local administration, and later sailed from Vladivostok to the United States. Later still, he arrived in London where he renewed contact with his fellow

16

18

17

revolutionary, Herzen. Tchernishevsky, by contrast, was more of a scholar and writer, but his message was no less revolutionary for all that. He was disillusioned with the serfs' emancipation of 1861. Soon after, he petitioned Alexander II with the warning of the danger of a peasant revolt. This, he said, could only be averted if men of education came together to exercise power in a constitutional manner. Soon afterwards Tcher-nishevsky was condemned to fourteen years' forced labour and deportation. Tchernishevsky's main legacy to the revolutionary movement was the vision contained in his famous novel, *What Is to be Done?* Here he depicted a life of personal freedom led by men and women in a commune where all property was publicly owned. The role of the state was limited to supplying the capital needed to run agricultural and industrial enterprises.

In 1881, the struggle between the government and the revolutionaries took a more drastic turn, when radicals assassinated the Tsar (20). This was the work of a revolutionary terrorist group known as "The People's Will." Some abortive attempts on the Tsar's life had taken place before 1881. The successful attempt was managed by Sophia Perovsky, the daughter of a senior govern-ment official. It was she who signalled to her fellow-conspirators the route of the Tsar's carriage through St. Petersburg. This pre-pared the four men, who were to throw the fatal bombs, to take up their positions. The first bomb stopped the procession (21), a second one killed the Tsar (22). The police very soon caught up with the conspirators. They captured all the six ringleaders, of whom

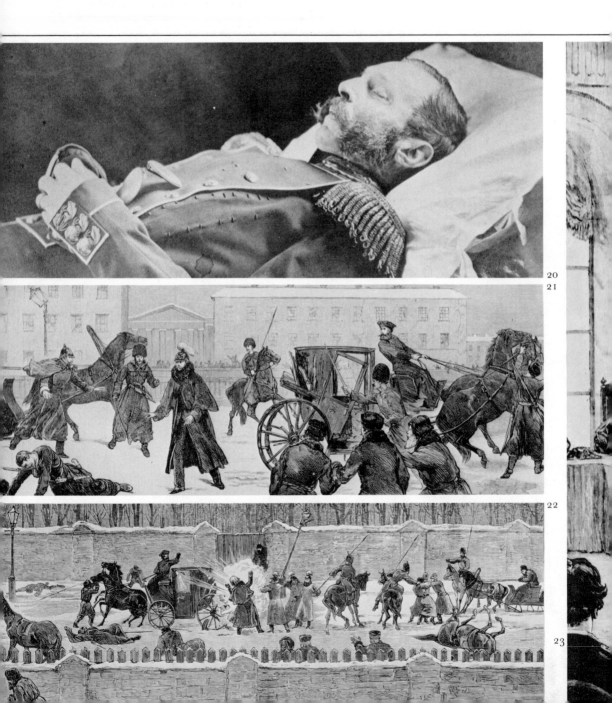

20
21
22
23

five were sentenced to death after a short trial (23). In other respects, too, the assassination was a political failure. The plotters had hoped to spark off an uprising amongst the peasants, but nothing of the sort happened. Moreover, not only was the terrorist group broken up, but Alexander III—the successor to Alexander II—proved much more reactionary than his father, and sought to undo some of his father's reforms. The policy of assassination was not entirely given up, but it was no longer so prominent. Not until the early 1900s was it fully revived. Meantime, in the unexpected calm that followed the assassination, there was a turn away from "populism" —with its reliance on the peasant—towards Marxism. This reflected the fact that industrialization was taking hold of Russia.

CHAPTER TWO

STRAINS OF MODERNIZATION

AT THE END of the nineteenth century Russia was still an agricultural country in the main. The first official census in 1897 showed that five-sixths of her 129·4 million people were peasants. Despite the emancipation of 1861, or perhaps because of the way in which emancipation was carried out, the peasants remained poverty-stricken and were in many respects second-class citizens. A partial exception were the Kulaks—the wealthier peasants—who could afford to employ other peasants. As time passed, the position of the peasants actually worsened because of the growth in their number. The wooden hand plough was still in use. When the peasants tried to rent additional land to cultivate, the competition among them forced up rents to an impossibly high level.

The government was not unaware of these problems, and tried to ease them in various ways. In the 1880s, for example, it reduced the taxation burden on the peasant. It also made it easier—although mainly for the Kulaks—to borrow money to buy more land, and encouraged planned migration to Siberia.

In reality, none of these measures helped very much. The peasants remained as poor as ever. On the other hand, it is also true that they did not stir from their political apathy. Despite all the activity and agitation of the revolutionaries, the peasants remained, as a rule, quiescent. No contrast is more striking than that between the miserable living conditions of the peasants and their lack of interest in political matters. There were exceptions of course—during the Crimean War, for example—but these did not disturb the general picture. Nor were they any guide to what might happen if the peasants should become really aware of their poor position.

In the meantime, a more dynamic source of discontent was developing within the Empire. This was a consequence of industrialization and the growth of an industrial working class. In 1891 the government began to intensify its efforts to modernize and industrialize Russia, to drag the country into the twentieth century. The pace was rapid. Results soon began to show in a vast expansion of the railway network, and in the coal and iron industries of the Donetz, Dnieper, Moscow, St. Petersburg, and Polish regions. The oil deposits at Baku were exploited and the textile industry grew by giant strides. The new railway network served both strategic and economic purposes, with special reference to the lines that connected the grain producing areas of the interior with growing ports such as Riga and Odessa.

The government wished not only to develop Russia's resources, but also to equip the country to face competition from the other great powers. In fact, was Russia a great power at all? After all, the country had failed in foreign policy all through the nineteenth century; its agriculture was backward, subject to recurrent failures of the harvest; and its industry was almost non-existent. There was every incentive to develop the Empire's unused resources in manpower and raw materials. Great obstacles faced this policy. Opposition was voiced by the defenders of agricultural interests; the bureaucracy was weak, both at a local and national level; Russian businessmen were hardly enterprising; authority was distributed amongst several different, and often conflicting, organs of the State; and the country lacked a technically trained élite.

Russia's economic growth was purchased at a price. In essence, it meant adding a new source of discontent to a social system that was already very uncertain of itself. This new problem came from the new industrial working class who entered the factories and workshops of Russia's industrial revolution. They were still small in number in the 1890s, but their importance came from the fact that they were concentrated in a few major cities such as Moscow and St. Petersburg. Moreover, the size of the industrial proletariat was growing as industry itself developed. The workers' wages were low; there was very little effective factory legislation limiting the hours or conditions of work. Because most of the workers were peasants, newly arrived from the countryside and unused to modern machinery, there

24

was a high rate of industrial accidents. Many of these workers were more used to the primitive wooden plough (24). Altogether, it was very hard for the former peasant to acclimatize himself to urban life, where all his skills were useless; and he was simply not used to the contrast between the need for strict timekeeping in the factory and the easy-going ways of the village. As a consequence, the peasant-worker was far less likely to accept the factory and its ways than he had been prepared to accept equal hardship in his native village (25, 26, 27). With industrialization, a new period had opened in Russian history, and it would be a far more dangerous one than ever before.

26 This new industrial age in Russian history is known justifiably as the "Witte period." It lasted roughly from 1892 to 1903 and is named after the dominating figure of Sergei Yulievitch Witte (28), the Minister of Communications during that period. Witte was an ambitious and capable administrator. He dreamed of rescuing Russia from dependence on uncertain harvests, of realizing the potential of his country's resources, and so enabling Russia to play a part in world politics that Witte thought was its due. The key to all this was industrialization, and particularly improved communications through the development of railways. A line under construction is shown here (29). The railway industry still remained very primitive, as can be seen from these pictures of a composite train on the Iranavka railway (30), and a railway station at Porochavaya (31). Even so, the railway

28

network was expanded very rapidly, and opened up Siberia and the Trans-Caspian territories through the construction of a line from the Caspian Sea to Samarkand (32). Money was obtained through governmental loans and private investors. Similarly, foreign firms were encouraged to come and set up business in Russia, as in the Kharkov textile mill (33) set up by Messrs. Hume and Lister of England. But foreign capitalists wanted high dividends on their investments. Witte's policy of rapid industrialization also involved higher indirect taxes on such everyday items as sugar, paraffin, matches, tobacco, and liquor. Only in this way could the Russian state acquire enough revenue to pay off its debts abroad. These indirect taxes in their turn raised the workers' cost of living. The towns were full of street beggars (34).

28 The workers in the new factories and workshops sometimes lived in poor shanty-town dwellings, as in this example from pre-revolutionary times (35). Even if employers built special hostels for their women workers, as shown in this dormitory for workers in a Moscow textile mill (36), the premises were hideously overcrowded and insanitary. Feeding arrangements were often limited to open-air soup kitchens (37), or to doss-houses (38).

If one recalls that wages were low and the exploitation of labour unrestrained, then it is easy to understand why clashes with the police were so frequent. Moreover, the workers were forbidden to strike, or to form trade unions or any collective organization. However, strikes did take place, and in many cases were accompanied by severe government repression. A notable example was that at the famous Morozov textile factory in Vladimir (39). The

35   37
36   38

local governor called in troops and police to quell the workers. A later inquiry revealed such serious abuses by the management that the government enacted improved labour regulations. But they had little effect. At the end of the century the authorities formed in the factory districts a special police force that could be rushed to trouble spots, as required. In fact, this force was insufficient and troops had to be used more and more often; 19 times in 1893, 33 times in 1900, and 500 times in 1902. An even more disturbing symptom of industrial unrest was the growing number of the strikes which were politically motivated. The workers were striking not merely for a higher wage, but also in order to overthrow the system of government which denied them their basic human rights.

30 At much the same time as an industrial proletariat grew up in Russia, so did the first Marxist groupings. These were the followers of Karl Marx (1818–83) (40) who saw society in terms of an irreconcilable conflict between the middle class of employers—the capitalists who owned property—and the working class who owned nothing except their labour power. In Russia, Marx's theories seemed out of place; the peasants far outnumbered other groups, and the middle class was very weak. On the other hand, because of Witte's policy of industrialization, the numbers of both middle class and working class were undoubtedly increasing. The father of Russian Marxism was G. V. Plekhanov (1857–1918) (41). In his youth, Plekhanov was a member of the group of revolutionaries who had assassinated Alexander II. But he lost faith in terror as a means to political revolution, and

40 41
42 43

44

in the supposed revolutionary potential of the peasants. As a result, Plekhanov became converted to Marxism. He went into exile in Switzerland and there, together with Vera Zasulich (42) and Paul Axelrod (43), he founded a small party in 1883 called "Group for the Emancipation of Labour." The nucleus of Russian Marxism had been formed. Of course, it had as yet no real political importance, although similar Marxist groups appeared in Russia itself. "The Russian revolution will triumph as a proletarian revolution, or it will not triumph at all," Plekhanov told the Second Communist International Congress in Paris in 1889. A Russian cartoon of 1901 depicted six layers of Russian society: the Tsar, the ministers, the clergy, the army, the middle class, and the proletariat (44).

The most important new Russian Marxist in the 1890s was Vladimir Ulyanov, better known to history as Nikolai Lenin. He is the man with whom the whole Russian revolution is unchallengeably identified. A Russian painting shows Lenin talking to a group of peasants (page 43). Lenin was born in 1870 at Simbirsk in the Middle Volga region. Here he is shown as a young child (45). His father was a school-teacher who rose to become Director of Schools in the province of Simbirsk; his mother, too, was a school-teacher. They raised a large family. Lenin is seated bottom right (46). At school Lenin did well; he was "exceptionally talented, constantly diligent and accurate." It seemed that before the young boy lay a distinguished career. However, he was already feeling politically dissatisfied. This feeling grew when his elder brother Alexander was executed in 1887 for plotting to assassinate

45   46   47

48   49

the Tsar. Although Lenin was revolutionary-minded, he disagreed with assassinations, and in this idealized picture by a Russian artist he tells his mother that there must be another way (48). Lenin studied law at the University of Kazan but was soon expelled with other students for rioting. He became a student at the University of St. Petersburg where he finally graduated. Already he was active in secret Marxist discussion groups in Moscow (47 *centre*). But in 1895 he was arrested and spent the next five years in prison and in exile. But these years were not wasted. He studied Marxist theory, and wrote an important work on the rise of capitalism in Russia. Lenin's character and political hopes were formed by this time. He was a man of simple habits whose fixed aim was to bring Communism to Russia and to the world. This photograph of Lenin (49) was taken in 1900.

The contrast with Lenin's fixed resolve was embodied in the new Tsar, the last of the Romanov dynasty, Nicholas II. Nicholas succeeded his father Alexander III and was crowned in 1896. The new reign began with a disastrous omen. During the coronation celebrations in Moscow so great was the crowd that panic broke out. In the resulting stampede more than 1,200 people were killed (50). However, celebrations in Moscow next year went off more peacefully, as in this view of an open-air banquet (51). The new Tsar was a great family man and loved to be photographed with his children, aboard the royal yacht for example (52). He also liked the company of military men and is shown here with a group of army officers (and some members of the royal family) (53). The Tsar's qualifications were not appropriate to the time. The Empire was replete with unsolved problems,

stemming from the state's many new burdens in industry, agriculture, and foreign affairs. But all these problems passed the new Tsar by, despite his undoubted devotion to his duties as he saw them. Perhaps the Tsar's greatest fault was his determination to rule as an autocrat. At his accession he coldly dismissed as "wild dreams" the hopes of certain well-wishers that they, too, might have some say in the work of government. The Tsar's inflexibility might not have been too risky if only the Tsarist autocracy had been efficient. But it manifestly was not. One British diplomat at the court even said that Russia had "no real government." Each minister acted on his own, "doing as much damage as possible to the other ministers." This was no system to face the storms of the twentieth century.

35

51

53

52

CHAPTER THREE

THE CHALLENGE OF THE TWENTIETH CENTURY

IT WAS NOT LONG before the new century revealed its full threat. There was, for example, a revival of student assassination in 1901 and 1902 when the Ministers of Education and the Interior respectively were killed. In 1902 disorder spread to the peasant world, in particular to the provinces of Poltava and Saratov. In Saratov the harvest failed, and in the absence of government help the peasants took the law into their own hands. They ransacked the landowners' granaries and even seized land for themselves.

Agitation among the workers paralleled that of the peasants. In Zlatoust, a Ural mining centre, sixty-nine workers were killed before troops succeeded in restoring order. But the most momentous movement took place in south Russia and Trans-Caucasia. Workers in railway workshops, oilfields, and engineering plants went on strike in an enormous area stretching to the north of the Black Sea and the Crimea and into the Ukraine. All the evidence shows that in 1903 the strikes, demonstrations, and mass meetings were on a larger scale than ever before. Sometimes they were so vast that the government's orders were of no avail against the massed might of the workers.

Another index to the troubled state of the country was the fact that parts of the country were more often coming under emergency administration. Ordinary civil rights were suspended; a citizen could be arrested without trial, or his home searched by the police. In 1903 the secret police compiled a report which showed that public opinion was dominated "by the unusual growth of the anti-governmental, oppositionist and social-revolutionary movement, and equally by the measures taken by the Russian government in the struggle against this movement."

What did the workers want? Why were they striking? In the main it was not for political reasons; they were not opposing the government. They were hoping for better conditions of life and work. They wanted, for example, the introduction of a working day limited to eight hours, an increase in wages, better treatment by their foremen and supervisors, factory schools for their children, and free medical aid. In these circumstances, there was inevitably a revival of political activity, most of it illegal.

The turn of the century saw three different types of political organization join the struggle against Tsarism. At this time the most dangerous was a liberal movement of opposition. This was formed of diverse social groupings. They ranged from liberal-minded landowners to professional men such as teachers, doctors, engineers, academics, and lawyers. They were not revolutionary in the sense of seeking to overthrow the social order. But they definitely wanted to end the political monopoly of the autocracy. The liberals called for "the political liberation of Russia" and for the establishment of a democratic régime. This would be based on the principle of elections that would be universal, equal, direct, and secret. In the social sphere the liberals gave first place to the welfare of the workers.

The second grouping took the name of Socialist-Revolutionary, known as S-R for short. The S-Rs were primarily devoted to the cause of the peasants. Apart from this, however, they did not have a well-organized outlook. Victor Chernov was their great leader. Chernov argued that a great peasant upheaval must come one day, in which the peasants would simply confiscate all the land that was not already under their control. This land would be made available to them according to their needs. The peasants would then either farm their land as small proprietors, or join in a peasant co-operative. This was the ultimate goal of the S-R movement. In the meantime, like the liberals, they demanded greater political liberty, an eight-hour day in factories and villages, and a constituent assembly representing the whole people and entrusted with the task of working out a new political system for the Empire.

What distinguished the political struggle of the S-Rs was their use of assassination. By killing leaders of the government—perhaps even the Tsar himself—they hoped to disorganize the government and, second, to stimulate the peasants to rebellion when they saw the prestige of the government so under-mined. This was a reversion to the policy of the terrorists of the 1870s and 1880s; it was not much more successful. Certainly, the peasants did rise against the land-owners, but this was because of their own specific grievances, not because of any act of terror, however spectacular.

The third group of anti-Tsarist politicians was that formed by the Marxists. By the early 1900s a number of groups existed throughout Russia, but not until a congress was held in exile in London in 1903 did these come together and actually form a party. Even now, however, there was little unity amongst the Marxists. They were divided between the Bolsheviks (from the Russian word meaning "majority") and the Mensheviks (from the word meaning "minority"). Lenin led the Bolsheviks. The dispute concerned the type of person entitled to join the party. Lenin saw the Marxists, and especially his followers, as a party of picked full-time revolutionaries, utterly devoted to the overthrow of Tsarism. But his opponents, the Mensheviks, preferred a larger and looser type of organization.

At the time these differences were bitterly fought out. But they had little practical importance. Far more important, as the stimulus to revolution, was the outbreak of war between Russia and Japan in January, 1904. Within a short time, this brought the Tsarist system of government almost to the point of collapse.

In February, 1904, war broke out between Russia and Japan because of their rivalry over Korea. This crisis followed several decades of friction between the two powers. The war was notable for the catastrophic defeats suffered by the Russian forces on land. The Japanese prints on these pages show the Battle of Keu Lein Chein (54) and cavalry engagements at Fang Huang Chein (55). The Russians suffered particularly heavily at sea. The hostilities began with a swift Japanese victory which destroyed the Russian Far Eastern fleet based at Port Arthur on the China coast. This was followed by the Japanese occupation of the port, shown by a Japanese artist in exultant mood (pages 44 and 45). London's *Punch* pictured the "Russian bear" at bay (56). The climax came in May, 1905, when the Russian Baltic fleet was destroyed. This fleet had sailed 18,000 miles around the

world from the Russian ports on the Baltic to the Far East where it hoped to engage the Japanese. It took seven months to reach Tsushima Strait, lying between Korea and Japan. There the Russian fleet met with disaster. The thirty-odd vessels were destroyed by the Japanese in a day and a half. Thousands of Russian sailors lost their lives in the catastrophe. An exultant Japanese caricaturist shows a Russian admiral presenting the Russian Emperor with some of the broken vessels (page 46). From the beginning, the war was unpopular on the Russian home front. The areas which first showed opposition to the war were the outlying parts of the Empire such as Finland, Poland, and the Caucasus. Underground political parties demanded an end to the autocracy and its replacement by a democratic system of government.

54

56

55

40 The Russian government itself suffered a staggering blow when Vyacheslav Plehve, the hated Minister of the Interior, was assassinated in July, 1904 (57). The correspondent of the London *Daily Telegraph* witnessed the assassination. He saw the Minister drive by in a closed carriage: "Then suddenly the ground before me quivered, a tremendous sound as of thunder deafened me, the windows of the houses on both sides of the broad streets rattled, and the glass of the panes were hurled on to the stone pavements. A dead horse, a pool of blood, fragments of a carriage, and a hole in the ground were parts of my rapid impressions. My driver was on his knees devoutly praying and saying that the end of the world had come . . . Plehve's end was received with semi-public rejoicings. I met nobody who regretted his assassination or condemned the authors."

57

"On the ruins of capitalism towards worldwide brotherhood of workers"—a Russian Communist poster of 1920 by Nikolai Kocherghin

The Decembrist revolt of 1825. This watercolour painting by
K. Kolman shows the mutiny on Senate Square, St. Petersburg
(from page 10)

The Russian revolutionary leader Lenin talking to peasants in
Shushenskoye village (from page 32)

The Russo-Japanese War 1904–5: a Japanese impression of the
occupation of Port Arthur (from page 38)

The Russo-Japanese War 1904–5: another Japanese view of the
occupation of Port Arthur (from page 38)

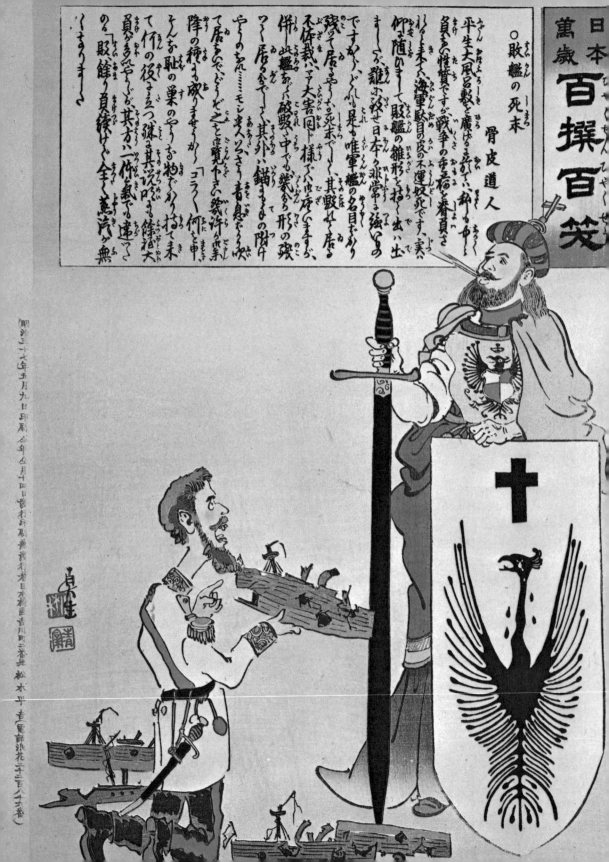

Above "Bloody Sunday." Tsarist soldiers shoot down the crowd of defenceless demonstrators under Father Gapon outside the Winter Palace in St. Petersburg on Sunday, 9th January, 1905 (from page 57)

Opposite The Russo-Japanese War 1904–5: a Japanese print showing a Russian admiral handing back broken ships to Tsar Nicholas II after the Battle of Tsushima (from page 39)

Above A defiant Russian worker sets fire to the pillars of the state: the Priest, Tsar, and Capitalist (from page 81)

Opposite Demonstrators shot down on "Bloody Sunday" outside the Winter Palace in January, 1905 (from page 57)

49

Haunted by the ghost of the French Revolution Tsar Nicholas II allows a glimmer of the Light of Progress into his chamber. From an American cartoon of 1905 (from page 62)

A Russian Communist cartoon of 1919 showing Rasputin at the
side of Tsar Nicholas II (from page 77)

The October Revolution of 1917: the attack on the Winter Palace in
St. Petersburg marked an important stage in the Bolshevik seizure of
power (from page 106)

Opposite left A Russian Communist cartoon showing Lenin sweeping kings, capitalists, and priests from the globe (from page 114). *Above* "Remember the starving"—a poster issued during the famine of the civil war in 1920 (from page 118). *Right* "You—have you enrolled as a volunteer yet?"—a Red Army recruiting poster of 1920

ИНДУСТРИАЛИЗАЦИЯ ПУТЬ к СОЦИАЛИЗМУ

56   "Industrialization—the path to socialism"—a Soviet poster of 1927
proclaiming the First Five Year Plan (from page 123)

In January, 1905, the very heart of the Empire, St. Petersburg, came under attack. Father Gapon (58) led a sort of government-sponsored trade union in the capital. When some of his followers at the giant Putilov factory in St. Petersburg (59) were dismissed for political activities, Gapon organized a great strike, and then a demonstration to petition the Tsar. The demonstration took place on Sunday, 9th January, 1905. At the head of a peaceful hymn-singing crowd, carrying icons and portraits of the Tsar, walked Father Gapon. When they reached the Winter Palace, troops fired heavily into the defenceless crowd. Perhaps as many as 1,000 people were killed or wounded (pages 47 and 48). "Bloody Sunday" sparked off the most bitter internal conflicts that Russia had ever known. Calls for vengeance came at the funeral of the murdered demonstrators (60).

58

59

60

During the spring and summer of 1905 the urban unrest continued: 80,000 strikers came out in April and more than 200,000 in May, to say nothing of endless protest meetings and demonstrations. Suspects were searched in the street (61), and arrested (62). Inevitably, the unrest spread to the countryside. In many places the peasants tried to take over and plough the landowner's estate. Police and armed guards had to hold off the peasants by force (63). But perhaps the most sensational evidence of collapse came from the Black Sea fleet. In June, 1905, the crew of its most modern battleship, the *Potemkin* (64), mutinied under the lead of a sailor named Matushenko (65, in white shirt). Initially they were protesting against poor food served in the men's mess. But when the Admiral ordered the shooting of thirty of the protesting seamen, the firing squad mutinied. The officers lost their

61

62

63

64 65

heads and before long the men found themselves in command of the ship. They were now uncertain what to do next. Eventually the *Potemkin* was allowed to put into the Rumanian port of Constanza on the Black Sea; there the ship was surrendered, and the mutineers were escorted ashore. This was a somewhat inglorious end to the mutiny. But it showed that the lack of official skill and control that led to repeated disasters in the Far East was leading to a similar result in the Black Sea. Later in November, 1905, the lesson was thrust home again by a mutiny at Sebastopol. Here the ringleader Lieutenant Pyotr Schmidt is shown under heavy guard (66). In May, 1905, after the defeats of Mukden and Tsushima, the Tsar's government decided to make peace with Japan. Fearing revolution inside Russia the Council of War decided that "internal order [was] more important than victory."

60 Russian and Japanese delegates met on board the American ship *Mayflower* at Portsmouth, New Hampshire. President Theodore Roosevelt of the United States mediated between the Russians on his right and the Japanese on his left (67). The delegates of each side are shown during an actual session. Witte, mid-right, led for the Russians (68). The peace terms, made in three weeks, naturally amounted to a heavy defeat for Russia. The cession of strategic points such as Port Arthur and the railway line from Port Arthur to Changchun, meant the end of Russian expansionism in the Far East. Peace brought no immediate relief. The strike movement and the incipient revolution reached their climax in October, 1905. The strike of railway workers (72) endangered the transport of troops on which the government depended for its security. From Moscow the strike spread to

67

68

69

70

71

the St. Petersburg printers and then to workers in other industries. Once again the students joined in. Here they are shown marching along the quayside in St. Petersburg, parading with the red flag of revolution (70, 71). The October movement had explicit political aims, *i.e.* to end the autocracy, although the strikers and demonstrators disagreed as to what should take its place. By the end of October Russia's entire railway system was virtually at a halt, and industry likewise. The police were helpless (69). At last the Tsar realized that he must make some concession to his rebellious subjects. Even now, it was only under Witte's urgent persuasion that the Tsar acted. The Tsar's "October Manifesto" gave the Russian people their civil liberties, and created an elected State Duma (Parliament) without whose approval no law could take effect.

The October Manifesto was a turning-point in Russian history. It signified some limit on the Tsar's power, and won over some of his more liberal opponents who were hopeful of more representative government. An American cartoonist of the day imagined the Tsar, haunted by ghosts of the French Revolution, cautiously allowing the light of progress into his chamber (page 50). However, the Manifesto did little immediately to calm the storm of revolutionary protest (73). In fact, it virtually coincided with the momentous formation of the St. Petersburg Soviet (Council) when some local workmen freely formed their own "parliament." It grew rapidly. Outside St. Petersburg more soviets sprang up. None achieved very much, but in St. Petersburg, for example, the Soviet did remain strong enough to defy the government. During much of October and all of November, 1905, the Tsar

73 74   75 76

had lost all his authority there. Not until early December did the cabinet dare to arrest the leaders of the Soviet. When it did so, the Soviet collapsed. But it had set an example of workers' militancy. In Moscow events took a different turn. Here the Soviet called a general strike, hoping for an armed uprising against the government. This desperate move failed (74) and the Government struck back with all its strength. It sent in regiments of Cossacks (75), and then bombarded the working-class district of Presnya (76, 77). Even now the Empire was not at peace. "In the localities of Livonia and Courland adjacent to Vitebsk there is complete anarchy," the Governor of Vitebsk reported to the Ministry of the Interior on 6th December, 1905. Brutal methods of repression were used. Witte restored order by seizing the villagers (78), and setting the huts of rebel peasants on fire (79).

77

78 79

CHAPTER FOUR

THE AFTERMATH OF 1905

TWO QUESTIONS ARISE from the events of 1905. First, why did the reformers fail, if opposition to the Tsar was so widespread? Second, what did the government learn from 1905? The answer to the first question is simple. Briefly, the government survived because its enemies lacked unity. The peasants were interested in securing more land and in ridding themselves of the burden of taxation. The workers, on the other hand, primarily hoped to win higher wages, improved living conditions for their families, and improved working conditions for themselves. The liberals, again, were far from blind to the social problem, but their main interest lay in achieving some sort of constitutional government. Some liberals were satisfied with the proposed Duma; others hoped to go further and make it a genuinely representative assembly. As for the revolutionaries, the S-Rs, Bolsheviks and Mensheviks, all pursued different aims by different methods.

Lastly, in the outlying regions of the vast Russian Empire—Finland, the Baltic provinces and Trans-Caucasia—the revolt against the Tsar was blended with the idea of national independence, or at least some form of national autonomy.

It is not at all surprising that the government should survive attacks delivered from such differing viewpoints. In any case, the attacks came at different times. Once the government had made peace with the Japanese in 1905 it was able, though not without some difficulty, to recall troops from the Far East to central Russia and deal with its enemies one by one.

Our second question—what did the government learn from its experiences in 1905—is harder to answer. It involves the policy of Pyotr Stolypin who became Chairman of the Council of Ministers in June, 1906. Stolypin came from the rich landed gentry. In 1905, as Governor of the province of Saratov in the Volga area, he was notorious for his ruthless suppression of peasant disorders. He continued this policy in office. In fact he issued regulations setting up special field courts-martial that ordered the execution of more than 1,000 victims declared to be guilty of disorder between August, 1906, and April, 1907. Ordinary courts-martial were no less active.

But this was only one aspect of Stolypin's policy. He also applied a policy of land reform to try to create a class of prosperous peasant farmers. He did this by making it possible for the enterprising peasant to leave the village commune to which he had formerly had to belong, and to consolidate all his scattered strips of land into one holding. This policy had some initial success, but the war with Japan made it impossible to proceed further.

Stolypin's premiership, which lasted until his assassination in 1911, also saw the infusion of capital into the countryside. A determined effort was made to raise the level of agricultural technique and productivity. Planned peasant emigration to Siberia took place, to reduce the demand for land in the over-populated provinces. All these measures undoubtedly helped to bring about a more contented peasantry. The improvement was further accelerated by the higher prices that Russian agricultural exports fetched on the world markets in the year before the war.

Unfortunately this happier situation was not matched in the political or the industrial sphere. This became evident from the time the elections to the First Duma were held in 1906.

66 The electoral system favoured the peasants and men of property. But the elections to the First Duma held in April, 1906, passed off peacefully (80) and the peasant delegates were elected (81). The Tsar himself opened the proceedings in the magnificent throne room of the Winter Palace (82), amid a scene of apparent harmony; troops paraded outside (83). But when the actual debates started in the Tauride Palace it very soon became clear that there was little, if any, common ground between the Duma and the Tsar's government (84). The primary reasons for this were the wishes of the Duma majority, led by the liberal Kadets. The Kadets wanted a much stronger and more effective say in the government. They also wanted more drastic treatment of the land question, even including

perhaps the forcible transfer of land from private estates to the peasants. On both these points there was no hope of compromise between the government and the Duma leaders. The Tsar decided to dissolve the Duma in July, 1906, barely three months after it had first met. The Second Duma lasted not much longer, from February to June, 1907, for the extremes of right and left were even more strongly represented. At this point Stolypin's government arbitrarily changed the electoral law; it reduced the representation of workers and peasants, and raised that of the urban bourgeoisie and landowners. As a result the Third and Fourth Dumas (1907–12, 1912–17) enjoyed more harmonious relations with the government. Photograph (85) shows Stolypin (upper right) with his family.

84

85

82

83

68 This harmony in the later Dumas was not, however, reflected in the industrial world. It is true that for a few years after 1906 the workers were far less strike-prone than they had been in 1905. But few of the workers' grievances had been put right. There always remained the chance of renewed outbreaks. Moreover, during the years after 1906 a fresh industrial upsurge took place which raised the number of workers from some 1·8 millions in 1910 to 2·5 millions in 1914. But the Stolypin reforms, which brought some prosperity to the peasants did not benefit the workers. For them food was scarce, homes overcrowded (87), and vagrancy widespread (86, 88). It is not surprising, therefore, that in 1910 the strike movement began to revive, usually led by spontaneous strike committees (89). In 1911 the movement grew stronger. Women and convicts were used as strike-breakers (90).

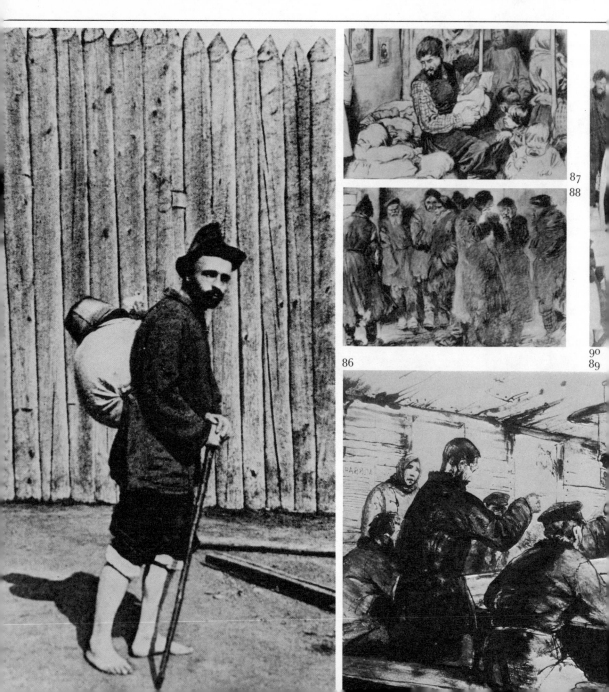

86

87
88

90
89

The new strike movement was largely the result of the massacre at the Lena Goldfields in Siberia. Here the workers lived in deplorable conditions, received a miserable wage, and endured a fourteen-hour working day (91, 92). They went on strike in February, 1912. The troops were called in and killed more than 170 workers and wounded 372 others (93). There was a tremendous rise in the number of strikers, coupled with an increase in Bolshevik influence amongst the workers. So serious did the situation become, that the Council of Ministers had to devote a number of special meetings in 1913 and 1914 entirely to the labour problem. They spoke of the "hostility and bitterness" between employer and workman, of the "irreconcilable" attitude of the workmen to the state. But the Council did nothing constructive to end the disturbances.

91

92

93

70 Before the First World War (1914–18) Russia, as we have seen, was far from united. In the Fourth Duma elected in 1912 Paul Milyukov (94), a leading deputy from the liberal Kadet party, said that the government and the Duma were "two hostile camps." Alexander Kerensky (95), a labour lawyer who represented peasant socialists in the Duma, said that the different Duma party leaders in 1914 were discussing "a federal democratic republic on the basis of radical social reforms." In 1914, such attempts were fruitless. But in 1917 these discussions helped towards the overthrow of the Tsar, and the policy of the next government. Meantime, a great Bolshevik-supported strike in St. Petersburg in July, 1914, marked the climax to the whole prewar strike movement. The slogans were: "For the eight-hour day! For socialism!" Fierce street battles with many casualties broke out between police and

94
95
96

97
98

workers. Red flags were unfurled, and make-shift barricades erected. But when Russia actually declared war on Germany in July, 1914, a great outburst of patriotism ended all internal conflict. Russian mobilization went well (96, 97, 98). Patriotic placards and propaganda of which this postcard is an example (99) helped to maintain popular enthusiasm. Even many former left-wing enemies of Tsarism supported the Tsarist war effort. Picture (100) is an official poster: "Everyone help our glorious soldiers! Subscribe to $5\frac{1}{2}\%$ loan!" Lenin, however, saw the war as a struggle among the capitalist powers, and hoped to convert it into a civil war. But he was in exile at this time, without much influence. His followers in Russia, including the Bolshevik deputies in the Duma, were systematically arrested. It was the First World War itself that brought revolution to Russia.

99

100

In the early months of the war Russia rendered great services to the Allies. Her advance into East Prussia in the autumn of 1914 forced the Germans to divert troops from the Western front, and this played a vital part in saving Paris from the German advance. A Russian artillery column is shown on the move in 1914 (101). But the next year the Russians had to pay a terrible price for their participation in the war. The German troops were able to advance deep into Poland, Lithuania and Galicia, in many cases against little opposition (102). The retreating Russians often evacuated or destroyed villages and food stores *en route* to stop them falling into German hands (103). But this also had the effect of creating a serious refugee problem. Refugees in vast numbers fled from the battle areas and seriously added to the congestion on already inadequate roads (104). Special arrangements had to be made

101

102

103

to feed the refugees, for example at this mobile kitchen in Petrograd (105). Sometimes the refugees were reduced to camping out in the woods (106). The Russian Minister of Agriculture said in July, 1915: "Refugees move in a solid mass, they tread down the fields, destroy the meadows and woods . . . The railway lines are congested; even movements of military trains and shipments of food will soon become impossible. I do not know what is going on in the areas that fall into the hands of the enemy, but I do know that not only the immediate rear of our army but the remote rear as well are devastated, ruined . . . It is in my competence to declare, as a member of the Council of Ministers, that the second great migration of peoples, staged by general headquarters, will bring Russia to the abyss, to revolution and to ruin."

The same incompetence that dominated the home front prevailed in the army. Soldiers were mainly recruited from the peasantry (107). Though hardy, they had little idea why they were fighting (108). Not only that, the government called up men in such large numbers that it could not provide enough arms for them all. Sometimes men had to salvage the rifles of their dead or wounded comrades. Even when the Russian troops did have mod-ern equipment, the terrain made it awkward to bring it into action, as in an attempt to take guns up the slopes of the Carpathian Mountains (109), or to drive lorries across muddy fields (110). The Russian officers were quite unable to cope with the demands of modern warfare. The Commander-in-Chief, the Grand Duke Nicholas Nickolayevitch (111), was popular with his men but by no means able to meet the demands of the situa-

107
108
109

110
111

tion. In these circumstances it is not surprising that the Russian troops suffered large casualties (112) and lost even larger numbers through capture by the Germans (113). In 1915 the Germans took Warsaw and Vilna. The Allies did their best to make up for the shortage of Russian equipment. But the Empire was easily blockaded, and such ports as Murmansk and Archangel had very poor rail contact with the interior of the country. The line from Murmansk to the capital, which was renamed Petrograd at the beginning of 1917 because St. Petersburg sounded German, was only completed during the war itself. Incredible mismanagement prevailed at Archangel. There was such a lack of storage facilities that packing cases literally sank into the soil owing to the sheer weight of the stores piled up on top of them.

2

113

One feature of military life in 1915 and 1916 was the growing number of deserters. These men had lost all faith in the capacity of their officers to lead them, in the value of the government's war aims, or in any idea of discipline. In such cases it was often necessary to restore order by force (114, 115). Military defeat and confusion on all fronts inevitably jeopardized the standing of the government. Thousands of Russian soldiers were taken prisoner (116). In the summer of 1915, in fact, industrialists and politicians were already saying that "the days of Tsarism are numbered . . . the revolution is now inevitable." In the Duma a broad "Progressive Bloc" of members from many parties came together to urge Tsar Nicholas II to form a new government "which would enjoy the confidence of the public." Nicholas refused any political change that would limit his autocratic powers.

114 115

116

The public and politicians also condemned the Tsar for the influence wielded at the court by a wandering "man of God," Gregory Rasputin (117). Rasputin in two Communist posters exercises an evil influence over the Tsar and Tsarina (118 and page 51). High-born ladies of society appreciated Rasputin for his supposed hypnotic powers and often entertained him (119). Rasputin was assassinated by his enemies in the winter of 1916. But they could not deal so easily with the other ills and problems that beset the Empire. By now, even the secret police said the "Russian state life is at present threatened by the unrelenting approach of a grave shock." The police based this conclusion on the growing number of strikes, and on the depressed state of morale in the towns.

117

119
118

CHAPTER FIVE

THE MARCH REVOLUTION 1917

IN PETROGRAD at the beginning of 1917, the strike movement, hunger, military defeat, governmental chaos, incipient industrial breakdown, administrative confusion—all created a truly revolutionary situation. Pleas, warnings, threats assailed the Tsar. "Unrest grows; even the monarchist principle is beginning to totter," wrote Grand Duke Alexander Mihailovich. "I repeat once more—it is impossible to rule the country without paying attention to the voice of the people, without meeting their needs." When Buchanan, the British Ambassador, had his last audience with the Tsar in January, 1917, he warned him that he had come to "the parting of the ways . . . The one will lead you to victory and glorious peace, the other to revolution and disaster . . ." A British visitor in Petrograd early in February, 1917, found it "as certain as anything can be that the Emperor and Empress are riding for a fall. Everyone—officers, merchants, ladies—talks openly of the absolute necessity of doing away with them." When a general from the front spoke to a meeting of Duma members he told them that the army would joyfully welcome "the news of a *coup d'état* . . . A revolution is imminent and we at the front feel it to be so. If you decide on such an extreme step, we will support you. Clearly there is no other way . . ."

In this atmosphere of universal distrust and hostility, the slightest spark could trigger off an open revolt. This situation was reached in February, 1917. Within a matter of a few days, the party leaders in the Duma formed themselves into a provisional government, with Prince Lvov as Premier. The Tsar abdicated. Suddenly, after more than three centuries of rule, the Romanov dynasty had ceased to govern Russia. It happened so quickly and easily that it was hard to realize what it actually signified. In time to come the supporters of the Tsar would regroup, but not just yet. The revolution began in Petrograd, but it spread rapidly throughout Russia. Five per cent of the garrison troops were given short leave to carry the news to the villages. Nowhere did it meet very much opposition. The old Tsarist order had let itself become so unpopular that it collapsed almost of its own accord. So far, at any rate, few people were willing openly to demand the restoration of the Tsar. Almost none of his spokesmen dared to make a stand.

Yet when people stopped wondering at the rapid collapse of the Tsarist system, they were faced with a major question: who now ruled in Russia? Who, or what, had taken the Tsar's place? A provisional government had been formed of the various party leaders in the Duma. But this Duma had been elected on a very narrow franchise and was quite unrepresentative. Moreover, from the outset the provisional government had to share power with a new Soviet in Petrograd. This was a rebirth of the Soviet that had come into existence in 1905. Then, it had survived for only a few weeks; but in 1917, in conditions of freedom, it went from strength to strength. The question might very well be asked: who was more powerful—the provisional government or the Petrograd Soviet?

Here was an inherently unstable situation. It was all the more so as the war, and the tremendous political changes inside Russia, had made millions of normally apathetic people take an interest in politics. The question facing the revolution was this: in what direction would those newly awakened masses move?

The crisis began to develop in Petrograd from the end of February, 1917. The first signs of trouble were riots caused by food shortages. The hungry queues became desperate, as in this Russian artist's picture. The sign reads: "No Bread" (120). The International Woman's Day on 8th March brought thousands of discontented and hungry people into the middle of Petrograd (121). Tsar Nicholas II ordered General Khabalov, in Petrograd, to disperse the demonstrators by force. But even some of the garrison troops mutinied. On 12th March, Khabalov wired to the Tsar, "I cannot fulfil the command to re-establish order in the capital." The mutiny spread in a flash to virtually the whole Petrograd garrison. On 11th March the city had 600 mutineers, on 14th March 170,000. A Bolshevik eyewitness saw the front ranks of the crowd come closer and closer to a cordon

120

of soldiers: "Women, with tears in their eyes, were crying out to the soldiers, 'Comrades, take away your bayonets, join us!' The soldiers were moved . . . The next moment one bayonet is slowly raised, is slowly lifted above the shoulders of the approaching demonstrators. There is thunderous applause. The triumphant crowd greeted their brothers clothed in the grey cloaks of the soldiery. The soldiers mixed freely with the demonstrators."

"There is no government any longer," exclaimed Mikail Rodzyanko (122), the President of the Duma. A crowd demonstrated outside the Duma with banners inscribed "Land and Freedom" (123). A painting by I. Vladimirov recreates the days of the February Revolution (124). The defiant worker seemed ready to set fire to the three pillars of the state—the Tsar, the priests, and the capitalists (page 49).

121

122

123 124

The leaders of the Duma had not wanted matters to go this far. Despite their contempt for the Tsar and distrust of his government's ability, they had hoped to maintain some continuity and perhaps have the Tsar's brother, Grand Duke Michael, rule as Regent. But Michael refused and the Duma leaders had no choice but to form themselves into a provisional government pending more settled constitutional arrangements. The leaders of the government were Prince Lvov (Premier), Milyukov (Foreign Affairs) (125), and Kerensky (Justice) (126). The provisional government followed a very liberal policy in internal matters, and issued news sheets to the crowds outside (127). It introduced the eight-hour day (though not everywhere), released political prisoners, abolished capital punishment and exile, instituted trial by jury for all offences, and ended all discrimination based on religion,

125
126

class, or national differences. Full liberty of conscience, worship, and the Press, were also introduced. Within a few months, in the spring of 1917, Russia became the freest country in the world. As it was only a provisional government, it also promised to call a constituent assembly, representing all the Russian people, to devise a permanent government. But did all this put the government on a firm footing? The answer is "No." It still remained weak. "The old [governmental machine] had disappeared, the new was not yet established," wrote Kerensky. Lastly, the new government still continued the war against Germany. This was to become its greatest source of weakness. Photographs below show Russian artillerymen in their trenches (128), German soldiers handing over letters for prisoners of war (129), and a Russian unit during a difficult retreat (130).

27 129
28 130

While the provisional government pursued its legislative policy, the atmosphere in Petrograd was joyous. The problems of social and political life still lay in the future. Soldiers in the garrison cheerfully went over to the revolution (131) or paraded with revolutionary posters (132, 133). Soldiers and workers joined together in welcoming the institution of the eight-hour day (134). Crowded public meetings were held at which, for the first time in Russian history, full and free expression of views was permitted (135). Those days in early March were the honeymoon of the revolution. Crowds celebrated the birth of

liberty by breaking open police stations and releasing the inmates, tearing down the imperial insignia from the law courts and other buildings (136). They marched through the streets singing, and welcomed back political prisoners from exile. Almost overnight, a multitude of spontaneous bodies came into existence, political clubs, trade unions, co-operative associations, and cultural societies. The most important of these were the Soviets throughout the country, and the most important Soviet of all was that at Petrograd.

131

132 133
134 135

136

The mutiny of the troops (137) and the rapid collapse of the Tsarist government had surprised left-wingers in Petrograd as much as anyone else. But on 12th March, some thirty to forty of them recovered from their surprise and decided to organize a new Soviet on the model of that established in 1905. They hastily appealed to the people of Petrograd to elect their deputies to the Soviet, one man for every 1,000 workers per factory, one man for each factory with less than 1,000 workers, and one soldier for every company of soldiers. The Soviet first met on the evening of the 12th with about 250 people present. They elected an Executive Committee whose Chairman was Nikolay Chkeidze (138), a Menshevik, and issued the famous Order Number One whereby the soldiers would only obey the provisional government so long as there was no conflict with the Soviet's policy. At one

stroke, therefore, the Soviet deprived the government of much of its possible support. The new Premier, Prince Lvov, complained that the government had "authority without power" and the Soviet "power without authority." The Petrograd Soviet grew in numbers—here it is shown in session (139)—and claimed the allegiance of hundreds of thousands of people. But it was only one of thousands of lesser soviets throughout the country—among peasants, workers, and soldiers (140). Nearly all were dominated by Mensheviks and S-Rs. But there were also a few Bolsheviks who tried to increase their influence. These Soviets were all elected by the people in the area where they functioned; discussion in them was entirely free. In March and April, 1917, all Russia seemed to be engaged in a vast discussion of political reforms and future hopes.

137

138   139

140

The March Revolution surprised Lenin as much as anyone. He was anxious to turn the "imperialist" war into a civil war. Germany helped Lenin and other revolutionaries to return from Switzerland to Russia, as depicted in this painting (141); "Germany must create in Russia as much chaos as possible," said one German diplomat, if Russia were to be defeated. Lenin arrived in Petrograd in April, 1917 (142). So far, his party had taken no real share in destroying Tsarism. Inside the Bolsheviks' villa headquarters in Petrograd, Lenin called for a unifying policy of revolutionary action (143). First, the end of the Tsar did not mean that the revolution was over. Lenin hoped that Russia might undergo a further revolution, and herald a world socialist revolution. Second, Lenin entirely rejected the Russian war effort. Third, the Bolsheviks must encourage in the thou-

141 14

143 14

142

sands of soviets in Russia an all-out resistance to the provisional government. On the land question, Lenin called for the expropriation of all large estates, and the nationalization of all land. The biggest problem was the war, which caused the first serious clash between the provisional government and the Petrograd Soviet at the end of April and beginning of May, just when jubilant May Day demonstrations were taking place in Petrograd (144, 145). The provisional government was backed by Britain, France, and the United States, Russia's allies in the war against Germany and Austria. Naturally alarmed at Russia's weakness, they were somewhat reassured when Foreign Minister Milyukov promised to keep the Tsar's foreign policy of carrying on the war. On this basis, the provisional government received the good wishes of leaders like Lloyd George (146).

146

However, public opinion in Russia violently opposed any identification with Tsarism. Foreign Minister Milyukor was actually forced to resign. He was replaced by another liberal Kadet leader, Michail Tereshchenko, but this made no basic difference. However, the Minister of War also resigned. In the government reshuffle, five new ministers, Mensheviks and S-Rs, entered the cabinet. For a few days in mid-May, there was an acute political crisis which revealed the precarious political state of the country. The confusion in political circles reflected the great problems that the provisional government inherited from the Tsar. These could now find open expression in the new system of freedom. Thus soldiers could now demonstrate on the streets (147), some of them with socialist banners (148, 149). At the first All-Russian Congress of Soviets in June, 1917, Lenin could

149
150

147
148

talk openly about seizing power from the government (150). He was not taken seriously at this time; most of the delegates were Mensheviks and S-Rs who were represented in the cabinet and co-operated with the government. But within a few months the balance of power would move towards the Bolsheviks. A major reason for this was the government's slow, almost stagnant, agricultural policy. The policy was discussed even in the village assembly (151). Actually there was little to discuss, since the conflict of interests between peasants and landholders made any progress almost impossible. From April, 1917, onwards the peasants began to loot the manor houses (152), cut down the landowners' timber, graze their cattle on their pasture, and seize their implements. Rural disorders were so widespread that the authorities were unable to intervene.

151

152

But if the provisional government was weak at home, it certainly tried to live up to its obligations in foreign policy. This was shown in the immense effort devoted to making ready a military offensive against the German and Austrian troops on the Russian western and south-western fronts. This was mainly the work of Kerensky who was now Premier and Minister of War. Kerensky was photographed with General Alexeyev, the Russian Chief of Staff (153). Kerensky and the Russian officers had an uphill task before them. More than anything else, after suffering so many defeats and casualties, the Russian troops wanted peace. These men, for example, are cheerfully making their way back home from the front (154). This unit on the south-western front has just voted, "Down with the war!" (155). In these unpromising circumstances, Kerensky and the officers had to persuade the army that an

153 154

15

156

killed (162). There is still some mystery as to the true cause of these "July Days." Was it part of a Bolshevik plot to seize power? Was it a spontaneous reaction of the masses to the weakness of the Soviet, as they saw it, a reaction encouraged by eager Bolsheviks? Whatever the real causes, the government itself had no doubt that Bolshevik subversion was at work. Just as the demonstrations were petering out, the government published a series of documents alleging that Lenin was behind them. They suggested that the Germans had commissioned him "to use every means in his power" to agitate for a speedy peace with Germany. This *Punch* cartoon supported the suggestion: a Bolshevik with German gold tries to seize the Russian maiden, as the Kaiser looks on (163).

159

162

160

163

The immediate sequel to the "July Days" and the government's accusation of treason by Lenin, was catastrophic for the Bolsheviks. Lenin himself had to flee to Finland, with false identity papers made out in the name of K. P. Ivanov (164). Another temporary loss to the Bolsheviks was that of Leon Trotsky, who was forced underground (165). He had returned to Russia from exile earlier in 1917, and within a month or two threw in his lot with the Bolsheviks. Trotsky's talents as orator, pamphleteer, and military leader were to be of enormous help to the Bolsheviks. He quickly became Lenin's closest collaborator. For the present, however, the government took advantage of Bolshevik unpopularity to ransack the party's headquarters. It stopped the Bolshevik newspaper *Pravda* and brought in regulations

164
165
166

that authorized subversive publications to be closed down. It outlawed appeals to violence, and banned all marches and demonstrations. In these circumstances Lenin decided that the Bolsheviks must change their policy. He dropped the slogan, "All Power to the Soviets," and no longer saw any hope "for a peaceful development of the Russian revolution." There was no middle way open between a military dictatorship on the one hand, and "the transfer of power into the hands of the proletariat supported by the poor peasantry to put into execution the programme of our party" on the other. In Lenin's absence, Joseph Stalin expounded the new policy to a party conference (166).

It seemed that the Bolshevik left-wing danger to the government had been thwarted, but now a danger from the right emerged. This was identified with General Vladimir Kornilov, Commander-in-Chief of the Russian armies (167). Kerensky (168) sensed the danger and accused the General of wishing to make himself a dictator. Kornilov sought "all civil and military powers" and wanted to restore a system "opposed to the conquests of the revolu-tion," said Kerensky, and ordered Kornilov to give up his command. Kornilov flatly refused. Instead, he dramatically ordered his troops to march on Petrograd; his followers took a solemn oath of allegiance (169). This pro-duced a dramatic change in the situation. The Petrograd Soviet had always been suspicious of Kornilov, and now it organized the Petro-grad workers into armed defence squads. Factories produced arms and ammunition for

167 168

169 170

171

the workers. Volunteers dug trenches and built barricades to defend Petrograd. Sailors from the Kronstadt naval base moved in to help. Railwaymen diverted trains, blocked the lines, and removed the rails. Others went to meet those cavalrymen who supported Kornilov, and convinced them not to attack the capital. A special "Committee for Struggle with Counter-Revolution" was formed of Bolsheviks, Mensheviks, peasant deputies, and S-Rs.

The Committee co-ordinated all these measures. So well did the Committee do, that the Kornilov movement failed before it had really started. Many of his troops were at a loss (170). No fighting ever took place. Kornilov himself and a number of his Cossack colleagues were taken prisoner, and his army disintegrated (171). Kerensky remained Premier, but of a government with even less power than its predecessor.

CHAPTER SIX

THE NOVEMBER REVOLUTION
1917

AS THE AUTUMN of 1917 approached, it brought with it ominous signs that the social and economic problems that had undermined Tsarism in February were not being solved. For all its good intentions, the provisional government had not been able to overcome such vital difficulties as food supply. In the countryside a collapse of law and order affected almost all Russia. Almost every important area of rural Russia was subject to upheaval. The central agricultural and middle Volga provinces were particularly disturbed. The western provinces of Minsk, Pskov, and Mogilev also suffered. The peasants systematically encroached on all the landowners' rights in their estates. They pastured their own cattle on private land, they violated cornfields, hayfields, and forest plantations. They drove away the landowners' servants and hired farmworkers, and stole the landowners' timber stocks.

Initially, the aim of the peasants was to seize land and property. Their next objective was to make it impossible for the landowners and their families to remain on their estates. The peasants used actual physical force to drive out the landowners. One report of events in the countryside said that "the peasants are destroying the manor houses, driving out and ill-treating the owners and their servants and burning the buildings . . ." From the province of Ryasan came a report that every day in the first half of October saw the destruction of between three and five manor houses.

These happenings in the countryside only showed one side of the virtual breakdown of authority, and the almost complete loss of control by Kerensky. From many urban and semi-urban localities came reports of food riots, the looting of shops and wine stores, arson, destruction of land records, and attacks on prisons. The government in Petrograd was almost completely isolated from the people it sought to govern.

Ominous reports came of similar conditions in the army. There was no longer any pretence of fighting the Germans. More and more deserters made their way back home from the front to share in the village seizures. Food stocks, equipment, and clothing all began to run out. Reports from every front poured into headquarters describing "complete lack of confidence in the officers . . . The influence of Bolshevik ideas is spreading very rapidly. There is a general weariness, an irritability and a desire for peace at any price." In the Twelfth Army, reports asserted, "an intensive agitation is being conducted in favour of an immediate cessation of military operations on all fronts. Whenever a whole regiment or battalion refuses to carry out a military order, the fact is immediately made known to other parts of the army through special agitators."

On the western front, because of general war weariness, bad food, and mistrust of officers, "there has developed an intense defeatist agitation accompanied by refusals to carry out orders, threats to the commanding personnel, and attempts to fraternise with Germans. Everywhere one hears voices calling for immediate peace, because they say, no one will stay in the trenches during the winter . . ." On the south-western front, the reports said: "The Bolshevik wave is growing steadily, owing to general disintegration in the rear, the absence of strong power and the lack of supplies and equipment. The dominant theme of conversation is peace at any price and under any conditions. Every order, no matter what its source, is met with hostility . . . The position of the commanding personnel is very difficult. There have been instances of officers committing suicide . . . The soldiers are engaging in organizing armed invasion of the surrounding country estates, plundering provisions . . . of which there is a scarcity in the army."

Naturally, these conditions found political expression in a swing towards the political extremes. The Kornilov movement on the right wing was one example of this. On the left wing it was paralleled in growing support for the Bolsheviks. When elections for the town councils at Moscow and Petrograd were held in the early autumn, for example, they showed a tremendous swing in public opinion towards the Bolsheviks. In Moscow they even secured an overall majority as compared with the combined votes for the Mensheviks, Kadets, and S-Rs. In certain soviets the same pattern was repeated. A notable example of this took place in the Soviet at Kronstadt, an important naval base near Petrograd. Here the sailors showed unmistakable sympathy for the Bolsheviks and their supporters. But it was in the largest and most important Soviet of all, that of Petrograd, that the most dramatic change took place.

In the autumn of 1917 it was becoming clear that the main social and economic problems remained. Long queues of hungry women gathered for bread that never came (172). Soldiers' wives protested against their inadequate rations (173). The breakdown of transport was accentuated (174). A famous *Punch* cartoon showed "Anarchy" waiting to strike the Russian maiden (175). "German Gold" is feeding monarchy, but this is certainly a simplification. The provisional government did not seem to be making headway. In the second half of September a tense debate took place in Petrograd involving Bolsheviks against the other parties. Leon Trotsky has left a vivid memory of the scene. As the voting took place, he recalled, "there was the utmost imaginable tension . . . All understood that they were deciding the question of power . . . In every corner of the hall an

172

impassioned although whispered agitation now began . . . The arms of an unseen balance were oscillating." The voting figures showed a Bolshevik victory. "The new majority applauded like a storm, ecstatically, furiously," Trotsky wrote. He himself was at once elected chairman of the presidium (the governing body of the Soviet). Outside Petrograd, many less important Soviets recorded similar swings towards the Bolsheviks. So far as policy was concerned, all demanded the end of the Kerensky government, an end to the war, and a new land distribution. Of course, many soviets throughout the vast Empire were still loyal to the Mensheviks and the S-Rs. But those soviets controlled by the Bolsheviks all lay in key areas, not only in the major cities of Petrograd and Moscow, but also in industrial areas and big garrison towns.

174 175

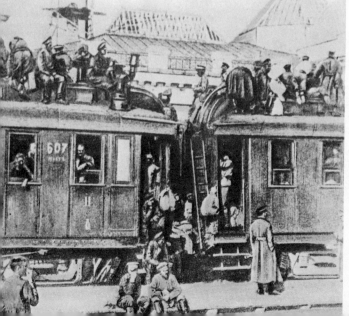

Lenin decided that the Bolsheviks must now make a supreme bid for power. Although he was still in hiding in Finland (176) messengers kept him informed of events. Through helping to defeat the Kornilov movement the Bolsheviks had won back much of the sympathy lost in the "July Days." Thus Lenin urged the Central Committee of the Bolshevik party to plan at once for an armed uprising. "Having obtained a majority in the Soviet of Workers' and Soldiers' Deputies in both capitals, the Bolsheviks can and must take power into their own hands," he wrote on 25th September. Many of the Central Committee thought this a reckless and premature demand, but eventually Lenin won them over. The Central Committee took the fateful decision on 23rd October. Disguised, Lenin went secretly to Petrograd. He wore a red wig to cover his bald head, and shaved off his

176 177

178

179

beard. For ten hours the Committee members argued whether the time was really ripe for an armed uprising. In the end they agreed, although they did not fix a precise date. Lenin returned to Finland and the others hurried to prepare the uprising. Trotsky was the brilliant planner of the Bolshevik revolt, ensuring that his supporters were well armed and trained. He formed a Military Revolutionary Committee (M.R.C.) to co-ordinate these activities.

This sent commissars to all the Petrograd regiments and authorized the city arsenals to arm the workers. Factory meetings were held in Petrograd to whip up the workers' enthusiasm (179). Other groups of workers were given arms and taught how to use them (177, 178). These were the troops of the imminent revolution. Trotsky and the M.R.C. finally decided on the night of 6th/7th November as the moment to strike.

As the great city of Petrograd went to sleep that night, a force of armed factory guards—the Red Guards—troops and workers went into action. They occupied the main post office, the Telegraphic Agency of Petrograd, the bridges over the River Neva running through the city, the state bank, railway station, power station, telephone exchange (180). Next day Trotsky issued a poster asserting that the provisional government was overthrown, and that power had passed to the Military Revolutionary Committee on behalf of the Petrograd proletariat and garrison. This claim was in fact premature. Not until the evening was the Winter Palace taken by direct assault (181). Many paintings celebrated the storming of the Winter Palace. One (pages 52–53) depicts the scene at the Palace gates. That night, Smolny, once an exclusive girls' school and now guarded by men of the Red Army,

180
182

181
183

184

an internal security and police force (the *Cheka*), was the scene of the Second Congress of Soviets (182). Delegates attended from soviets throughout Russia. But they also had their own party-political allegiances, which gave the Bolsheviks a slight majority over the Mensheviks and the S-Rs. The Bolsheviks now had the confidence to form a government composed entirely of members of their own party, the Council of Peoples' Commissars. Lenin, who had just returned from hiding, presided. First, he invited all the First World War powers to declare an armistice and open peace talks. Second, he abolished all private land ownership in Russia. These decrees caused great excitement when read out to the troops (183). But more than declarations were needed to keep the Bolsheviks in power. A painting by M. Sokolov depicts Lenin at work at Smolny (184).

CHAPTER SEVEN

THE BOLSHEVIKS IN POWER

ACCORDING TO THE BOLSHEVIKS the proletariat was in power. This message they proclaimed throughout Russia. But was this really the case? In 1917, and perhaps even more so in 1918, Bolshevik power was very fragile.

Certainly, when Lenin declared an end to the fighting and made armistice proposals, and when, furthermore, he decreed the nationalization of land, he satisfied two overwhelming demands. He had fulfilled his promises of peace and land. But his third promise, bread, had yet to be redeemed. This was not the only problem the Bolsheviks faced. The collapse of transport and communications, the breakdown in industry, the absence or shortage of daily necessities— all these were equally pressing problems.

Indeed, danger threatened the Bolsheviks from all sides. A close observer of events in Petrograd in October and November, the great diarist Nikolay Sukhanov, thought that no more than 500 disciplined men could have overthrown the Bolshevik power. "All were against them," said John Reed, a sympathizer from America then in Petrograd, "businessmen, speculators, investors, landowners, army officers, politicians, teachers, students, professional men, shopkeepers, clerks, agents. The other socialist parties hated the Bolsheviks with an implacable hatred. On the side of the Soviets were the rank and file of workers, the sailors, the undemoralized

soldiers, the landless peasants and a few— a very few—intellectuals."

Opposition to the Bolsheviks showed itself in various ways. Many sections of the Civil Service went on strike, for example post office workers and telephone operators. Bank clerks also went on strike; the railway workers' trade union refused to co-operate with the new government; a group of army officers attacked the Petrograd telephone exchange; a number of patriotic committees were formed to defend the Fatherland; and nationalists in such areas of the former Empire as the Caucasus and the Ukraine were striving to break loose and set up their own independent states.

Outside Russia, the Bolsheviks had to confront the hostility of Britain, France, and the United States. These were, or at least, had been, Russia's allies in the war against Germany. They had given a certain welcome to the March Revolution in the hope that it would be able to wage war more successfully than the Tsar. But this hope was not fulfilled. Even worse from the point of view of the Allies was the fear that socialism and general left-wing radicalism would spread from Russia to their own war-weary and hard-pressed populations.

This was perhaps a longer term fear. But in the short term the Allies feared an even greater danger: when Russia under the Bolsheviks started to negotiate peace with Germany early in 1918, the war on the eastern front virtually came to an end. Britain and France feared that Germany would not only transfer troops from the eastern European front to western Europe, but would also seize the vast stocks of arms and equipment that the Allies had sent to Russia, and which now lay in store at such ports as Murmansk and Archangel. Germany might also be able to make use of resources of food and raw materials from Russia which Germany gravely lacked, for example oil and wheat. But not until the end of 1918, when the war in the West was over, did Britain and France intervene actively against the Bolsheviks. During the rest of 1917 and most of 1918 the main danger to the Bolsheviks, political and economic, came from inside Russia itself.

Lenin took active steps to deal with this internal threat. He established the Red Army and brought in a range of measures to maintain economic power. For ex-ample, he nationalized the banks and the major industrial concerns, suppressed hostile newspapers, and abolished the old system of law courts. Conditions were so chaotic at this time that many of these measures had no effect at all. Nevertheless, this policy did serve to show that, by contrast with the provisional régime, Russia at last had a government determined to govern.

Lenin's most successful measure in the winter of 1917–18 was the formation of a coalition with the left-wing S-Rs. He brought some of their members into his government. This not only gave the Bolsheviks some support from the peasantry which they had previously lacked; it also weakened the main body of the S-Rs. This party provided some of the main opponents to the Bolsheviks. However, the two problems immediately facing the Bolsheviks came from the Constituent Assembly and the Germans.

Before their rising in November the Bolsheviks had again and again demanded the election of a Constituent Assembly. This Assembly would represent all the Russian people, and determine a new constitution for the country. After repeated delays the Assembly was at last elected early in December, 1917. Voting took place in an orderly fashion in most districts, as at this polling station in Petrograd (185). About 36 million people voted, but only one-quarter supported the Bolsheviks. This gave the Bolsheviks 175 seats out of the total of 707. Their allies, the Left S-Rs, won 40 seats. Even in combination, therefore, these two parties were far outnumbered by the S-Rs who won 370 seats. This gave them an absolute majority. Russia had voted for socialism but not for Bolshevism. The Bolshe-

185

viks were so displeased by this result that they dispersed the Assembly. It held its first and only meeting in January, 1918, in the Tauride Palace in Petrograd. The building bristled with soldiers and sailors armed by the Bolsheviks. The S-R majority rejected a Bolshevik motion calling upon the Assembly to recognize the new Bolshevik government. At that the Bolsheviks and their friends withdrew. The rest of the delegates went on making speeches into the early hours of the next morning. Then the guards simply told them they were tired and it was time to go home. This meant that the Assembly was adjourned, and the next day it was dissolved. A possible focus of internal opposition to the Bolsheviks had been successfully removed.

During these proceedings in Petrograd, the Bolsheviks were at grips with an external enemy far more powerful than the S-Rs—the German invading forces. Fighting had ceased, for all practical purposes. The Russians had long been unable to fight, and the Germans were for the moment content to observe the continued social break-up of their enemy. Wounded Russian soldiers returned home from the front (186); German troops occupied Minks in 1918 (187). But the Germans still preferred peace and so quickly accepted Lenin's offer of an armistice. Negotiations were begun in January, 1918, at the Polish town of Brest-Litovsk. Trotsky headed the Russian delegation (190). The Russians wanted to make the negotiations last as long as possible; they hoped that revolution would break out in Germany and Austria. In fact they were already distributing pamphlets and

186
187

newspapers among their "German brethren" (188). The Germans, on the other hand, hoped for peace as soon as possible in the East. In the West, fresh American troops were pouring into France, and Germany could not keep her armies in eastern and western Europe at the same time. Germany also needed supplies of food and raw materials, which were available from defeated Russia. The two teams of negotiators are shown in session at Brest-Litovsk (189). The eventual peace treaty was one of the most ruthless in history. It took away from Russia about a third of its population, a quarter of its total area, and about half of its industrial strength. But from the Bolshevik point of view it at least had the merit of securing a breathing space; the revolution could now prepare for imminent civil war.

188
189

190

The civil war in Russia gradually began to break out towards the end of 1918 and the beginning of 1919. Lenin feared, on the one hand, that Britain, France, and Germany would join together in an assault on the Bolsheviks. On the other hand, he believed more than ever that the revolution would spread from Russia to the rest of Europe. He saw the collapse of Germany and the abdica-tion of the Kaiser; he saw the dissolution of Austria-Hungary; he saw everywhere social disruption and he thought that all this heralded a revolution in the West, as shown in a Communist cartoon (page 54). This hope offset the fear of a combined assault by Germany and the Western powers. As Lenin put it: "It seems to me that our present posi-tion with all its contradictions can be expres-

sed thus: firstly, we were never so near to the actual proletarian revolution as we are now; secondly, we were never in a more dangerous position than we are now." An early casualty of the fighting in Russia was the deposed Tsar Nicholas II and his family (191). In July, 1918, the Bolshevik base at Yekaterinburg (now Sverdlovsk) in the Urals was threatened by anti-Bolshevik forces, known as the Whites.

Here the ex-Tsar and his family were interned in the Ipatiev house (192). When the White Russians approached, the imperial family were taken to a downstairs room (193) and killed there by the local Bolsheviks. It was feared that if they remained alive they might serve as a focus of resistance to Bolshevism.

In the subsequent months, civil war flared up in four main areas on the outer fringes of Russia. To the south, the Ukraine, the shores of the Black Sea and in the Caucasus; to the east Siberia; to the north the ports of Murmansk and Archangel; to the west Estonia, not far from Petrograd (194). In all these areas former Tsarist army and navy officers took over remnants of their troops, helped by political enemies of the Bolsheviks, and fought against the newly established Red Army. In some cases, the Whites set up their own anti-Bolshevik governments, but these never lasted very long. On the Bolshevik side, Trotsky dominated the civil war (195). He displayed outstanding powers as a strategist and leader. He dashed from front to front in an armoured train, using his oratorical powers to inspire the new Red Army with fighting spirit. Soldiers were recruited into the Red Army

194

Annexed by Turkey 1918
Annexed by Rumania 1918
Pre-revolutionary Russia, Independent Republics from 1918
Non-Russian anti-Bolshevik forces
Russian anti-Bolshevik Generals
Positions of anti-Bolshevik armies August 1918
October 1919
May 1920

Anti-Bolshevik forces controlled Trans-Siberian Railway from Kazan to Vladivostok

Miles 0 100 200 300

Tsar Nicholas II and his family murdered by Bolsheviks 16 July 1918

(196, 197), and some of the first Red Army units were formed (198, 199). The worst danger for the Bolsheviks came in 1919. In March, White officers commanded by Admiral Aleksandr Kolchak in Siberia almost reached the Volga River, but by the end of April the Bolsheviks had checked the advance and Kolchak's men had to retreat (201). A little later the White officers in the north drove southward from Archangel, planning to unite with the armies of Kolchak which were advancing from the east, but this move failed. Nor did anything come of the later White attacks on Petrograd. This campaign produced a remarkable Bolshevik poster: "Shoulder to shoulder in the defence of Petrograd" (200).

197 198

199

200 201

The end of the civil war in the second half of that year brought with it a certain internal stability. But also tremendous social and economic problems, too. Perhaps the greatest of these problems was hunger, the theme of grim posters (page 55). Soup kitchens had to be established in the larger towns to feed numberless starving children (202). At open-air markets, local people bartered precious private possessions for even more precious supplies of food (203). However, in the famine in the Volga region in 1921 such palliative measures could not prevent a major catastrophe in which millions of people died. Economically, the picture was scarcely brighter. The years of war, and then civil war,

had left Russian industry paralysed, agriculture ruined, and communications disrupted. In addition to everything else a terrible inflation ruined the currency. In 1922, for example, railway fares were one million times as much as they had been in 1917. Internationally, however, a slightly brighter picture existed. The Soviet régime was at least accepted by the outside world. Certainly, no other country had followed Russia into Communism. On the other hand, many of the capitalist states had come to realize that they must come to terms with the new system. In fact, in 1921 two such major capitalist powers as Britain and Germany signed trade treaties with Russia.

202 203

CHAPTER EIGHT

THE SECOND REVOLUTION

THE BOLSHEVIK STATE had survived its enemies at home and abroad, but it by no means bore out the hopes of its leaders. On the contrary, because of the very weakness of the state, the Bolshevik rulers actually had to make certain concessions in contradiction of their own policies. One particular factor that forced them on this path was the outbreak of peasant revolts in various parts of Russia in the early part of 1921.

Because of the many practical difficulties, Lenin introduced what was known as the New Economic Policy (N.E.P.) in the spring of 1921. The object of N.E.P. was to push ahead with industrial reconstruction as fast as possible, without worrying too much whether this took place in strict accordance with Communist ideals. Above all else, industry must be restored to full activity. Lenin hoped to achieve this by following a softer policy towards the peasants, and by permitting a small amount of individual enterprise in trade and manufacture.

During the years of civil war the Communist state had requisitioned the peasants' surplus produce in order to feed the workers and soldiers. Under N.E.P., however, the state no longer seized the peasants' surplus grain. Instead it imposed a food tax. The peasant was now allowed to sell his surplus produce more freely to the townspeople, for as much as he could obtain. With his earnings he could also rent additional land, engage other peasants to work for him, and buy agricultural machinery. All this meant a revival of private enterprise in the countryside, and was very welcome to the peasants.

The same kind of private enterprise policy was also applied to industry. Small factories, for example, that employed fewer than twenty workers were returned to their former owners. But all large factories (as well as heavy industry, the railways, the banks and foreign trade) remained under the ownership of the state. Money regained some of its former value and the practice of paying wages not in money but in food or clothing tended to die out.

N.E.P. was undoubtedly successful. In the 1920s the relationship between the government and the peasants markedly improved. In fact, the peasants began to profit so much from the new state of affairs that they were dissatisfied at not being able to obtain enough manufactured goods from the towns. The Communist leaders, on the other hand, began to fear the emergence of a class of wealthy peasants unsympathetic to Communism. Industry also benefited from N.E.P. Transport was helped by the import of a thousand locomotives from Sweden and Germany and by loans from Germany for the purchase of manufactured goods. The population in general felt more prosperous.

However, this comparatively happy situation could not be allowed to last. Not only did it present political dangers to Bolshevism, not only did it contradict Bolshevik theory, but it left Russia weak economically and militarily in a hostile capitalist world. Only if Russian industry were developed would it be possible to produce the equipment and material needed to withstand the strain of modern warfare. Moreover, only planned industrial development could provide a higher standard of living for the workers and so bring socialism nearer. The First Five Year Plan of 1928 was indissolubly linked with the name and career of Joseph Stalin.

Lenin died in 1924. He was photographed shortly before his death with his successor as leader of Soviet Russia—Joseph Stalin (204). Stalin was born at Gori in Georgia (205) in the house shown in (206). He is also shown with a group of fellow schoolboys (207 *centre*). In later years he joined the Social Democrats (the Bolsheviks) and led a number of raids on banks in the years before 1914 to raise funds for the party. He was in exile when the March Revolution broke out in 1917, but he was released and returned to Petrograd. At first he edited the Bolshevik newspaper *Pravda*. He played little part in the events of 1917. When the Bolsheviks seized power, however, he acquired great influence in the organization of the Bolshevik party. He was able to place his own supporters in the most influential positions. Lenin

204

knew this and feared it. In the will he wrote in his last years, Lenin warned that "Stalin has concentrated unbounded power in his own hands, and I am not sure whether he will always know how to use this power cautiously enough." Stalin is "too rough," Lenin added. However, these fears were not made generally known at the time, and after some confusion Stalin officially succeeded Lenin. Stalin saw the failure of revolution outside Russia and decided that Russia must concentrate its resources on building "socialism in one country." This policy gave further impetus to the drive for Russian industrialization. In 1928 this resulted in the First Five Year Plan. As a Soviet poster of 1927 proclaimed, "Industrialization—the path to socialism" (page 56).

207

5
6

No words can give a just description of the scope and sacrifices and achievements of the Five Year Plan. The main emphasis was placed on the production of energy and construction material: coal, oil, steel, electricity, timber, and cement: hence the magnificent hydro-electric power station at Tashkent, 1931 (208). Another important aspect of the Plan was the training of workers to handle modern machinery (209). Yet a third aspect was the employment of every means of publicity to arouse popular enthusiasm for the great Plan (210). The life of every Russian was affected, because many sacrifices had to be imposed on the population in introducing round-the-clock factory shifts, cutting the supply of consumer goods, and even exporting foodstuffs that were needed at home. Foreign currency had to be earned in this way to buy machinery abroad. The industrial side of the

208
209 210

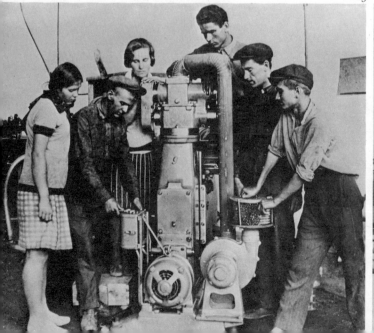

Five Year Plan was accompanied by a revolution just as great in agriculture. This transformed the system of individual peasant farms into a collective system of agriculture and required just as much re-education as in industry (211). This undertaking was as bold as it was breathtaking. Within a few years the habits of Russian peasants dating from centuries were violently destroyed and made to serve new collective aims. In some areas the opposition of the peasants led to a state of virtual civil war. It was in this way that the Bolshevik revolution can be said to have completed its first stage. By 1932, after many failures and achievements, it had shaped Russia into the Soviet Union we know today, which has earned a place as one of the great super-powers of the twentieth century.

211

FURTHER READING

J. Billington, *The Icon and the Axe* (London, Weidenfeld & Nicolson, 1966; New York, Knopf, 1966)

J. Blum, *Lord and Peasant in Russia* (New Jersey, Princeton University Press, 1961)

I. Deutscher, *Stalin* (London, Oxford University Press, 1967; New York, Oxford University Press, 1967)

S. Harcave, *First Blood* (London, Bodley Head, 1965; New York, Macmillan, 1964)

A. Herzen, *My Past and Thoughts* (London, Chatto & Windus, 1968; New York, Knopf, 1968)

L. Kochan, *Russia in Revolution 1890–1918* (London, Weidenfeld & Nicolson, 1966; New York, New American Library, 1967)

T. H. von Laue, *Witte and the Industrialization of Russia* (London, Columbia University Press, 1964; New York, Columbia University Press, 1963)

A. G. Mazour, *The First Russian Revolution* (London, Oxford University Press, 1966; Stanford, Stanford University Press, 1961)

W. E. Mosse, *Alexander II and the Modernization of Russia* (London, English Universities Press, 1970; New York, Collier-Macmillan, 1962)

J. Reed, *Ten Days That Shook the World* (London, Lawrence & Wishart, 1962; New York, International Publishers Co., 1967)

L. Trotsky, *History of the Russian Revolution* (2 vols.) (London, Gollancz, 1970; Ann Arbor, University of Michigan Press, 1967)

A. Ulam, *Lenin and the Bolsheviks* (London, Secker & Warburg, 1966; New York, Macmillan, 1965)

F. Venturi, *Roots of Revolution* (New York, Knopf, 1960)

H. Seton Watson, *The Russian Empire 1801–1917* (London, Oxford University Press, 1967; New York, Oxford University Press, 1967)

E. Wilson, *To the Finland Station* (London, Collins, 1960; New York, Doubleday, 1953)

PICTURE CREDITS

The Publishers wish to express their gratitude to the following for permission to reproduce the following black-and-white and colour illustrations: *Black and white*: The Trustees of the Victoria and Albert Museum, 54, 55; The Trustees of the British Museum, 14, 15; The Trustees of the Imperial War Museum, 100, 123, 127, 201; The Mansell Collection, 5, 6, 11, 16, 17, 28, 40, 52, 53, 56, 58, 60, 82, 87, 88, 91, 95, 96, 98, 99, 102, 103, 107, 108, 109, 113, 116, 119, 120, 124, 125, 128, 132, 142, 146, 152, 153, 157, 162, 163, 166, 168, 171, 175, 176, 180, 181, 185, 188, 189, 190, 193, 201, 203; The Radio Times Hulton Picture Library, 1, 4, 9, 10, 12, 13, 20, 21, 22, 23, 29, 30, 31, 32, 43, 50, 51, 57, 65, 66, 67, 68, 70, 78, 79, 80, 81, 84, 85, 90, 101, 104, 105, 106, 110, 114, 115, 117, 122, 126, 129, 130, 138, 143, 147, 151, 156, 165, 167, 169, 187, 191, 192, 195, 208, 210; Novosti Press Agency, 2, 3, 25, 27, 34, 35, 36, 38, 39, 46, 47, 49, 59, 61, 62, 64, 71, 72, 74, 75, 76, 77, 83, 86, 92, 93, 94, 97, 121, 131, 134, 135, 136, 137, 141, 150, 154, 158, 164, 170, 178, 179, 182, 183, 186, 197, 198, 209, 211; Tass News Agency, 18, 24, 26, 41, 42, 44, 63, 69, 89, 112, 133, 139, 140, 144, 145, 148, 149, 155, 159, 160, 161, 172, 173, 174, 177, 196, 199, 202; John Massey-Stewart, *frontispiece*; Pictorial Press, 7, 8, 45, 184, 204, 205, 206, 207; L.E.A., 73. Other illustrations appearing in this book are the property of the Wayland Picture Library. *Colour*: The Trustees of the British Museum, page 41; Novosti Press Agency, pages 42, 47, 48, 52–53, 56, *jacket*; The Trustees of the Victoria and Albert Museum, pages 44, 45, 46; John Massey-Stewart, page 55 *top*.